An Everyday Guy's Search for
America's Rare and Elusive Native Wildlife

GHOSTS

OF THE

WILDERNESS

DANIEL TOUJOURS

Ghosts of the Wilderness
An Everyday Guy's Search for America's Rare and Elusive
Native Wildlife
By Daniel Toujours

Published October 2023

Cover by Bia Shuja of Surviving Dreams.

All photographs within the book were taken by the author,
except for the black and white photograph of the Carrizo Plain
pictograph site from "Petroglyphs of California and Adjoining
States" by Julian H. Stewart, published 1929.

All events actually took place, but are not necessarily
presented in chronological sequence in order to fit a narrative
arc.

<u>Disclaimer</u>

This book recounts the author's personal experiences and approaches to outdoor activities and the author makes no warranties or representations as to the likely results or reliability of these approaches. This book makes no safety recommendations and is not a guide book. Solo hiking, travel through remote and rugged terrain, hiking in the heat, scrambling, and intentionally seeking encounters with wildlife are all inherently dangerous activities for which no amount of preparation can eliminate the risk. These activities should not be attempted without extensive, independent preparation and experience.

Those attempting any adventures or explorations do so at their own risk and should do their own research, follow all applicable regulations, obtain any needed permits, and leave no trace.

Although attempts were made to ensure the information presented in this book is accurate, this information should not be considered error-free, and the author makes no warranties, expressed or implied.

The author hereby disclaims and negates all other warranties.

"..walk, better yet crawl, on hands and knees, over the sandstone and through the thornbush and cactus. When traces of blood begin to mark your trail you'll see something, maybe. Probably not."

-Edward Abbey

Table of Contents

<u>Acknowledgements</u>

I'd like to thank my mom, my two brothers, my girlfriend, and my sister-in-law for supporting all my adventures and giving me the freedom to be myself. Thanks to my friends and colleagues for your support and presence in my life. Thanks to all the adventurers, explorers, philosophers, scientists, and artists for pushing the limits of the unknown, expanding what is possible, and inspiring us all.

<u>Prologue</u>

Palisade Glacier sits in a cirque carved from the Sierra Nevada mountains of California at approximately 12,400 feet of elevation. The cirque or cwm is formed from glacial erosion and is surrounded by four fourteeners, or mountains over 14,000 feet, creating the ambiance of an amphitheater. This is where I was attempting to go on that day in June.

"Sierra" means "mountain range" in Spanish. "Nieve" means "snow" in Spanish, and "nevada" here means "snow-covered". These are the snowy mountains, with enough snow to make Palisade Glacier the southernmost glacier in North America. But it's melting, fast, so I wanted to see it while I was still able.

I started just before dawn as an alpenglow created by the sun still below the horizon turned the mountains near the trailhead red. I began what would end up being a 22 mile day by hiking past turquoise lakes, their color created by fine glacially eroded particles suspended in the water column. At the moment, this water was making it possible for giant mosquitos to live here. Feeling in harmony with nature, I did not swat them away. This was their territory and I was only passing through. "Yes, feed, big girl." However, I quickly changed my tune and exploded into frenzied swatting. I needed to go higher to get away from these things. I came up with a song, moving from my lowest baritone to my highest singable pitch. "I need to go....high-uh-uh-er!!" You need to keep up your motivation and keep down your fear, somehow, when alone in these situations.

Finally, I reached Sam Mack Meadow just above 11,000 feet. From there it was all class 3 scrambling to the glacier viewpoint. I wasn't planning to actually walk on the glacier, as this carried an unacceptable risk to me of falling into a crevasse. I'd had experience with class 3 scrambling before this trip, but I was still learning to manage my fear of heights and slipping. On my trips into the wilderness, I take things as they come and see where I can find myself. Sometimes I go one step at a time farther and then maybe another step, always with safety in mind. "Let's see", I tell myself.

When scrambling, I use my hands and feet to move over the land. I ensure I have three secure points of contact before moving my fourth limb, I keep my body close to the slope or rock I'm moving over, and I test holds and contact points before committing.

I began to make my way along the standard route to the glacier viewpoint, which works its way around the left side of a slope. However, the route wasn't clear to me. I couldn't see my destination, since it was blocked by the curvature of the mountainside, and although I knew the direction, I wasn't sure how high or low on the slope I needed to be. I checked my GPS topographic map, but I couldn't get a precise enough location to give me confidence. Ten feet left or right on this slope would significantly change my elevation and I was concerned about going off course and getting "cliffed out", stuck on the mountainside and unable to advance or retreat.

Since there was no one else around to consult, I backtracked until I got to an upwardly sloping valley between two ridgelines, which I had flagged as a backup route to a glacier viewpoint before I headed out into the backcountry. Normally, this area would be covered in a snowfield, but recent warm weather had melted the snow on the lower portion. I began advancing up the slope until I reached the snowfield. From there, I put on my microspikes and began slowly making my way up the snowfield using my trekking poles for extra support. However, I couldn't get enough traction. I needed crampons, and I am no mountaineer. I exited the snowfield to the right and hiked up on bare ground to an area where the snowfield was the most narrow. I hoped to make my way across it there, but I again ran into traction problems. I slowly inched over to a boulder in the middle of the snowfield and climbed up so I could rest without worrying about slipping. The top of the boulder was covered with rock shards created through spheroidal weathering, and I cleared these away to make a place to sit. I pulled out my protein and energy bars in frustration, along with my baby food pouches, and started to plan my next move as I ate lunch.

Baby food pouches are my secret trick to getting extra nutrition on hikes and I like to go with vegetable-heavy varieties. Once, a cashier at the grocery store saw my pouches and asked, "Awww, how old is the baby?" "He's in his mid-thirties," I replied.

Suddenly, the remoteness of my location hit me. "Am I the first person to sit on this boulder?" I wondered. Perhaps I was at least the first person to sit on this particular layer of the eroding boulder. Inspired by the progress I had made so far, I began surveying the area with fresh eyes.

The left side of the snowfield came right up against a steep wall, and I initially dismissed using that route. However, I realized that I could return to the right side of the snow field, make my way back down to where the snow started, and return up the left side, skirting the edge with my left foot on the rocky slope, my right foot with my microspikes in the snow, and trekking poles in hand.

I set off and was able to use this technique to make my way clear of the snowfield. What a relief! From here it was all scrambling over boulders, which made up the entire mountainside. I set off using my three points of contact and testing each rock. This was particularly important because the rocks were porous, lightweight volcanic rocks, which could flip over and injure me. The rock scrambling continued for some time with no glacier in sight. At some point, one of the boulders I was stepping on flipped over, but my other points of contact kept me safe. I let out a half yell, half laugh born of adrenaline, fear, and my happiness that my technique had kept me safe.

Finally, the glacier came into view over the crest of the mountain I was traveling over. What a magnificent scene! The sound of flowing water was loud in the air as rivers of melted water flowed inside the glacier and a chunk of the glacier was in the slow process of calving off at the front end of the glacier where the ice and meltwater met. I took everything in and experienced the joy of being in a place I wasn't sure I ever would be.

Eventually, I began making my way back, but this time toward the standard route. I was able to see it more clearly from this direction, and soon I was back at Sam Mack Meadow. I stepped on rocks out into the middle of a stream of melted snow flowing down from the surrounding mountains and contentedly filtered and drank two liters of fresh, cold water.

Palisade Glacier

Introduction

Although I pursue many different types of outdoor activities and adventures, I like to think of what I do as "hiking", because it always is centered on moving over the land. In addition to my job and career, which I love and through which I can make a difference in the world, hiking has become a passion and a lifestyle for me. I hike routinely every week, all year round, and have covered thousands of miles in recent years. Camping and backpacking allow me to spend more time out there, or to be in the field for adventures at night or in the early morning. My activities mainly center around the American Southwest, which I define broadly as California, Nevada, Arizona, Utah, Colorado, and New Mexico.

Hiking allows you to see time. Sedimentary layers in rocks speak of long-vanished oceans and these layers may have deformed or tilted in the ages since deposition. A little knowledge about how various rock formations form can bring the past alive and give you a sense of your place in the flow of time. Artifacts connect you to people from the distant past. They are from a different time, but we share a common humanity. Although their way of life must have been so different, you feel as close to them as if they were an extended family member. You might even say a prayer for them.

Hiking allows you to experience profound silence, which contrasts markedly with the modern world. You might listen more and more closely, surveying what you can hear, but there is nothing. On other days, you might pick up on sounds you've never heard before. Once I was alone in a desert canyon and I heard a sound like a high-pitched fairy or pixie quickly flying past. I checked in with myself to determine if I was dehydrated, overheating, or hallucinating, but all was well. I soon realized this was the sound of a hummingbird's wings as it quickly flew past. In subsequent desert hummingbird encounters, I would realize they have a range of sounds, including a lower bumblebee-like sound.

With this silence comes solitude. It's not the solitude of escapism, all your problems and anxieties follow you out there. It's an opportunity to get to know yourself better, to become comfortable in your own company, and to work through your issues in order to become a more fully realized individual.

Hiking allows you to meet one-of-a-kind individuals. If commuting through traffic has destroyed your faith in humanity, hiking might restore it. There's no utopia of "nature people" out there, but many people you meet have worked hard and sacrificed in their own way just to be out there and pursue their passion. Interactions become more genuine and less formulaic. This might also mean respecting the boundaries of another person and realizing they may not be up for a chat. It also might mean carrying pepper spray to deal with the inevitable darker parts of nature, whether human or animal. (Note that bear spray is specially designed for defense against bears and is different from pepper spray in that it typically has a higher concentration of the active ingredient capsaicin, a larger volume, a longer range, and is more of a mist than a spray.)

Hiking allows you to interact physically and directly with the world around you in ways most modern humans are unable to do. Intuitions that you didn't know were there rise up from within you and you start to use a different type of intelligence. You come closer to the humanity of our ancestors. Perhaps their physical struggles have translated into our modern Four Types of Fun. I was told about these by a woman while huddled for protection from the wind in a rock shelter on a mountain peak just below 12,000 feet in Nevada. Type 1 fun is traditional fun, Type 2 fun is where you push yourself but would do it again, Type 3 fun is a challenge you're happy to have completed but wouldn't do again, and Type 4 fun you die.

Crafting my adventures and "hiking my own hike" has been a major creative outlet in my life, for which I'm very grateful. Some people speak of things being impossible, while others say anything is possible. I prefer a third approach. There are real barriers in life, which bring real pain, not everything is possible. However, we're often capable of far more than we realize if we commit to challenging ourselves.

Studies suggest the 7-repeat allele of the dopamine receptor D4 gene (DRD4-7R) is associated with novelty seeking, exploration, and discovery. Many of our ancestors may have been led to push to farther shores and new horizons by this variant, an essential societal role in humanity. If I have this variant, perhaps it would explain the "nature" side of my drive to get out there. The "nurture" side has been up to me and my background.

I've found my own way of mitigating risks associated with my adventures. If I'm traveling alone, as I often do, I leave my family with a detailed description of where I plan to be and when and let them know when I've returned. A shared online spreadsheet is a great tool for this. I'm always learning best practices and techniques and making sure I have the right gear. I carry a satellite personal locator beacon (PLB).

I believe there are many benefits to being familiar with the plants and animals in your area, the flora and fauna. It gives you a satisfying sense of place and a feeling of belonging. It allows you to have a relationship with the life around you. I enjoy identifying new plants and animals and seeing old favorites. But, I realized despite all my miles outside, there was some important American wildlife that had evaded me. This book recounts my search for that elusive wildlife. Along the way, we'll learn something about the history of these classic American animals and a little about their biology. I've also included human stories and history from the areas where I hike. Finally, I'll share some reflections inspired by my adventures. Perhaps sharing my stories can inspire a deeper connection to the natural world in your area.

This book is broken out into three sections: Deserts, Mountains, and Plains. Some of these categories might overlap, for example, there could be a mountain in a desert. However, I've grouped the stories in ways that make sense to me.

I didn't plan to write this book, but I found myself at a point where it made sense to do so. My intent is to write the type of book I would enjoy reading. I wish you a happy read and the best things in life. Don't forget to do good!

Deformed Sedimentary Layers

22

<u>Deserts</u>

The desert is one of my favorite environments, and I do not shy away from the heat. Growing up in the Midwest, I was used to hot and humid summers. In my hometown, when we returned to the car after doing errands in the summer, we had to be careful not to burn our hands on the seat belt buckles. When I moved farther southwest, I didn't think much about the heat. My thought was, "Of course, I'll head out in the heat. If I waited for perfect weather, I'd never be able to go anywhere." I also had this attitude toward the cold, but after decades of bitter Midwest winters, I had lost some of my enthusiasm for it. The "dry heat" of the desert with less humidity was also enticing to me.

Many people who love the desert refer to "desert season", the time of the year when the desert is relatively cool and more comfortable. However, I view myself as having a relationship with desert landscapes. In a loving human relationship, you are there for and with your loved one through good times and bad. I wanted to have a year-round relationship with the desert, and not restrict my visits to the "good times" of "desert season".

There's also something enjoyable about the heat, it's purifying. You're out there struggling to survive with the plants and the animals, connected to them. Life gets more simple, and you soon become comfortable with the environment and realize it's full of life and less desolate than you might have thought.

However, the desert is still a dangerous environment, and precautions need to be taken. When I see news stories of hikers who have died, the reason is often because they ran out of water. I hydrate beforehand and normally bring a gallon or two of water on my desert hikes, some of it chilled and in insulated water bottles with ice cubes. I can put this cold water or ice underneath my tongue where the blood vessels are close to the surface, and cool down my body. Fortunately, I've never had a problem with hyponatremia from drinking too much water or sweating too much, although I do plenty of both! However, some people take salt tablets or electrolytes to prevent this condition where blood sodium levels drop, which can lead to headaches, nausea, and confusion. I use lightweight, light-colored clothing that covers my entire body, including a neck gaiter I pull up over my face and gloves for my hands (these also help your grip on trekking poles and thicker gloves protect your hands from sharp, hot rocks while scrambling.). My top is a sun hoodie and I use a wide-brimmed hat with ventilation. I've even been known to put bags of ice underneath that hat. I attach a sun umbrella with a silver reflective outer layer and a dark inner layer to my pack when needed.

Once I was doing a twenty-some mile out-and-back day hike on a desert section of the Pacific Crest Trail (PCT), which runs across the Western US from Mexico to Canada. It's like a 3 foot wide, 2,650 mile long national park (although it is not designated as such and the land is managed by a variety of agencies, not just the National Parks Service, and even includes private land)! I was near the Mexican border, which is the starting point for most people attempting to hike the entire length of the trail. It was a hot day in the middle of a drought and toward the end of my "out" hike I ran into a man traveling the opposite direction as me who asked if I had any extra water. I wanted to help this man, but I wasn't confident that I could safely give up some of my water. Besides, there was a lake/reservoir a few miles up the trail in the direction he was heading. I knew a shortcut over a hill to decrease the distance to this lake to just over a mile while decreasing the total change in elevation and I pointed him in that direction (he had a water filter, but I did not). Hiking onward, I tried to conserve as much water as possible. On my return hike, I saw the man spread out under a tree past the spot where he could have turned off for the shortcut to the lake. He said he didn't think he could make it over the hill and seemed confused. I gave him a liter I had saved and stayed with him as he drank and recovered. He was soon more coherent and told me that he had flown out from the Midwest to hike the entire trail from Mexico to Canada. He was an experienced hiker and had hiked the Appalachian Trail in its entirety before, but he was surprised to find a stream he wanted to use as a water source on the PCT dried up and ran out of water. I soon found out he and I shared the same first name, used the same trekking poles, were the same age, and that he grew up in a town 30 miles away from where I grew up. I remember our school would have sporting and academic competitions with them! I wished him all the best on his journey, he said he would carry more water from each water source going forward, and he headed toward the lake.

This man was so similar to me, it seemed like he was an alternate version of me from another dimension coming as a warning about carrying enough water. I hope the man safely reached his goal of completing the trail. I worry whether I did the right thing, maybe I should have shared my water right away. In airline safety briefings before takeoff, they say that if the cabin loses pressure and oxygen masks drop from the ceiling, put on your own mask before helping others. By looking after your own safety first, you prevent yourself from becoming incapacitated, are then able to help others, and do not need help and become a burden for others. That's what I was trying to do when I encountered the man on that day. I later read a local news story of two hikers who ran out of water and encountered a mountain biker. The mountain biker gave them some of her water, only to run out of water herself and die from dehydration and heat stroke before she was able to return to her vehicle.

*

I was hiking on the far north side of the Anza-Borrego Desert in Southern California near where an ancient Cahuilla Native American village previously existed. The smell of the creosote bush was in the air and ocotillos stretched toward the blue sky. I was looking for pottery shards on the high ground near a dry desert wash where water intermittently flows. We might think of Native Americans of the past as living in perfect harmony with nature. However, interpretive signs in the more frequently trafficked part of the Anza-Borrego Desert State Park (although it's a state park, it's huge at almost 1,000 square miles) explain that Native Americans in the area were actually skilled manipulators of their environment, directing water through canals and reservoirs, clearing vegetation and replacing it with plants which created a more lush environment, and thereby surviving in this harsh area. The dry wash would have been regularly flowing and pots would have been used to carry water.

A Rare Red Ocotillo:
Normally the green ocotillo leaves fall off due to lack of water, but during especially wet years, cold weather in the fall and winter can turn the ocotillo leaves colors like autumn deciduous foliage.

I soon came upon a small brown pot shard. It could almost be mistaken as a rock flake, but closer inspection revealed this was made by human hands and fired. I was very happy with my find! I thought about who might have made the pot, who might have used it, and whether anyone had found the shard before me. I left the shard where I found it and continued toward a spring. If I had taken the pot shard, not only would it have been illegal, but I would have been depriving future people of the joy of finding it and connecting with its past. Maybe I would have enjoyed having the shard in my home for a few more decades, and when I had died hopefully my surviving relatives would know this was something special and might donate it to a museum. But, it might as easily be thrown in the trash. Archeological treasures are out there and still discoverable in many cases because people in the past found them and left them there. We should do the same for future generations. (As a side note, some archaeologists use the word "potsherd" as a way to distinguish archaeological findings from modern broken pottery shards.)

When I arrived at the spring, I found a bighorn sheep carcass not far away. This animal was killed by a predator, but which one? Coyotes are certainly in the area, but they are mainly limited to hunting bighorn lambs because of their size. No, this was a mountain lion kill. Mountain lions like to wait in ambush on cliff ledges or in brush, and this spring had both in the immediate vicinity. It would have been just a matter of time until an animal came for a drink. I have seen bighorn sheep climbing down rocky cliffs to access a water source in the past. The bighorn sheep carcass seemed to have been entered from the stomach, which is characteristic of mountain lions who seek minerals from the entrails. There were tracks around the carcass, which were somewhat indistinct but seemed to be from a mountain lion. Mountain lions normally cover their kill and return to feed over several days, but this carcass was uncovered. Perhaps in this sparse desert environment, there wasn't enough large vegetation to cover a carcass. Or perhaps the bighorn was small enough to be eaten in one sitting.

Mountain lions are protected in California, but as they face habitat loss and fragmentation throughout the state, they've pushed deeper into the desert. However, the peninsular bighorn sheep are endangered, and as much as I love mountain lions, I was sad to think that mountain lion predation might result in more bighorn deaths. I've seen conflicting studies about the threat posed by mountain lions to bighorns, and I'm not sure what is the right balance in protecting these two creatures or whether humans should even play a further role in this regard.

WARNING: THE NEXT PAGE CONTAINS A PHOTOGRAPH OF A BIGHORN SHEEP CARCASS KILLED BY A PREDATOR. PLEASE SKIP THE NEXT PAGE IF YOU DON'T WANT TO SEE THIS IMAGE.

Peninsular Bighorn Sheep Carcass (probably killed by a
mountain lion)

Hiking back from the spring, I saw Villager Peak towering above me from the desert floor and I remembered the remains of agave roasting pits which I saw on my last hike there. Villager Peak rises to an elevation of just under 5,800 feet and Cahuilla Native Americans would ascend out of the desert heat to harvest agave plants from higher altitudes where the environment is more conducive to their growth. They would roast them on-site in order to convert the starches to sugars and reduce their weight before transporting them back down. The process could have taken several days and they would use sandals made from the agave plant during their hikes and climbs. I was using modern gear when I was last on Villager Peak, but the hike was still a difficult one with rugged terrain and intermittent strong winds, so I can't imagine using agave sandals there. You would be hiking in still air one moment, and then you would hear a strong, swirling wind approaching. At one point, I ran to seek shelter behind a boulder and ducked behind it just in time for the wind to rush over my head above it. The environment changes from cactus to agave to pinyon pine trees as you ascend, so I can certainly see how a variety of conditions and temperatures might have contributed to those winds.

Back on the desert floor, I continued my hike out from the spring and came upon several Native American rock circles. There are several theories as to the purpose of these rock circles. Perhaps they were sleeping circles used to support protective structures made of vegetation or hide or perhaps they were used ceremonially. These rocks were arranged in broken circles with a spot for what appeared to be an entrance, which had the stone debris covering the area cleared and a worn path leading through the gap. It was amazing that these circles remained much as they were many years ago.

*

Stromatolites are structures formed by colonies of microorganisms that carry out photosynthesis, such as cyanobacteria, which look like layered piles of mud. These colonies were responsible for producing much of Earth's oxygen in primeval times and their fossils are found throughout the world. Modern stromatolites are rare, and only found in a few locations such as off the coast of Western Australia. However, Capitol Reef National Park in Utah has some of the largest known stromatolite fossils in Cottonwood Wash, which are normally approached from outside the national park by hiking into it along a narrow slot canyon carved into the earth by water.

The National Parks Service describes these fossils as "not easily accessible", however this doesn't provide much detail. Slot canyons are filled with sand, rocks, and boulders. This slot canyon is 1-6 feet wide at various points, so some of the boulders were stuck midway down and some were on the canyon floor. This requires scrambling over and under obstructions while contorting your body through small spaces at some points, and climbing up on the wall by "stemming" (putting hands and feet on opposite walls) or "chimneying" (putting your back on one wall and your two feet on the other) at other points. Depending on the time of year, and sometimes for much of the year, the slot canyon is also intermittently filled with water deep enough to require swimming, and this water can be very cold due to the lack of sunlight able to penetrate to the bottom of the slot canyon.

I find it amusing that the descriptions of hikes by land management agencies such as the National Parks Service, US Forest Service, Bureau of Land Management, and US Fish and Wildlife Service are sometimes imprecise or inapplicable. For example, the National Parks Service describes a Grand

Canyon Rim-to-Rim hike in a single day as not recommended, but a hike from the South Rim of the Grand Canyon to the Colorado River and back in a single day along the South Kaibab Trail as not possible. The North Rim portion of a Rim-to-Rim hike involves a longer distance and more change in elevation than the South Rim portion, so a Rim-to-Rim hike would seem to objectively be the most difficult. Also, many people have completed these hikes, so they're certainly possible. Nevertheless, I know these agencies are trying to provide warnings that are applicable to a wide variety of skill sets and experience levels and I've always found the employees of these agencies to have a genuine interest in helping you get outdoors, even if you have to use an older technology like a fax machine to send in your permit application. I've also found them to be very hardworking, not just from behind a desk, but physically getting out there and breaking rocks, clearing trails, and removing invasive vegetation, for which I'm thankful.

Hikers should consult multiple sources for information before heading out into the backcountry and ensure they have the skills, experience, and good judgment needed. However, reality doesn't always conform to the textbook, as the textbook is just a tool to understand reality. Guides might say that a certain plant flowers at certain times of the year and bears fruit at others, however I've seen flowers and berries on the same bush at the same time. Animal behaviors could be labeled and described, but you might see behavior that is novel. You might also see an animal outside its defined range. Media can only be a reflection of reality, and you've got to get out there to really see it. Perhaps that's why so many comment that their photographs from natural areas never do the landscape justice.

I started my hike into Cottonwood Wash at sunrise to allow for plenty of time. I was in a flow state, enjoying the landscape, until I came upon a couple considering how to get over an obstacle. The ground rose up in front of them to create a shelf and there was a large, smooth boulder wedged on the shelf high up and slightly overhanging the edge, but the walls of the canyon were too wide to touch both sides to stem or chimney. The couple tried several moves, but couldn't get over it, so I suggested stacking up rocks to create a foothold raised up a foot or so from the ground. However, all the rocks in the area were sandstone, which is lightweight and could potentially topple over more easily than other rocks. The couple didn't like that idea and turned back. I had almost broken my knee one time when a stack of sandstone rocks toppled over, but I wasn't ready to give up yet.

I collected sandstone rocks, each a couple of feet wide, and carefully stacked them up against each other and the wall so they locked in place as much as possible. I still couldn't get a grip on the boulder because it was so smooth, but there was a branch wedged behind it. If I pulled on the end of the branch, I was concerned it would snap due to a lever force, so I got a good grip on the thick bottom, tested it, and was able to pull myself up and get my right foot on a notch in the wall, and then put my left knee on the boulder. When I go up obstacles like this, I check out whether I can safely get back down (and vice-versa when I go down obstacles), because people can get trapped in situations like that. Climbing down is often more difficult than climbing up because your body can block your view of your feet. With a sigh of relief, I was able to move past the obstacle.

I noticed movement on the ground by a tiny creature not much larger than the size of my thumbnail. It was a red-spotted toad! These toads thrive in temporary pools and slot canyons in the desert and appear to come from nowhere. In fact, scientists used to think that animals such as toads, frogs, and some insects were produced by "spontaneous generation" from non-living materials. Instead, these toads wait underground, beneath rocks, or under wet vegetation for rain or other sources of water and when it arrives they become active, laying eggs in the water source. These eggs might be swept away in flash floods or killed by desiccation, but they hatch in a few hours. However, red-spotted toads themselves, despite being amphibians, are more resistant to desiccation than most organisms and are able to lose up to 30% of their body weight and rehydrate without ill effects. Nevertheless, they still require water. Red-spotted toads are able to absorb water through their skin, including absorbing trace amounts of water found in the sand. After only a few moments with the toad, it hopped away, and I bid it farewell.

Do you see the red-spotted toad?

I soon came to a boulder jam, where boulders as large as cars were wedged into the bottom of the narrow canyon. Rather than going over the boulders, I checked that the stones were securely in place and found a way under and then up through the middle of the jam. The final move to get free of the boulders required a serious twisting of my body, but I was able to escape the trap and escape injury.

Although still outside of the national park boundary, I came to a mile from where I thought the stromatolite fossils would be to find the slot canyon flooded with cold, dark water as far as I could see until the slot canyon curved away from me. I found some reeds and branches, which I used to probe the depth, and found it would require swimming. While I was prepared to get wet, the water was so cold that I thought it would be a dangerous risk of hypothermia to continue in the conditions, and I turned back.

Once I cleared the boulder jam again in the opposite direction, I was looking for a way to scramble up and out of the canyon to hopefully be able to walk on the surface at least as far as the national park boundary, if not all the way to the fossils. The topographic map showed rough terrain up there, and I wasn't sure if it would be passable, but I decided to try. However, every path I scouted or started up was covered with cryptobiotic soil crusts, which are formed of communities of microorganisms and help hold together the soil and prevent erosion-an important role in a landscape of sandstone. They look dark and spongy. They're prevalent in Utah and can take up to 50 years to recover if disturbed by footsteps. I've always respected cryptobiotic soil's role in the ecosystem and wasn't going to cause it any harm, so I stayed at the canyon's bottom and continued my hike out.

A red Indian paintbrush plant stands out among black cryptobiotic soil crusts.

After I made my way down the boulder high up on the shelf of land, I saw a young couple approaching me. I gave them all the "beta" I had learned on my trip down the canyon. Like a father, I warned them about the lightweight sandstone rocks and the tree branch. I told them about the cold water and said that I couldn't find a safe way past it, but maybe they could. This was only their second slot canyon, but I could tell they took what I was saying seriously. They said they had met someone coming out who told them the canyon was completely dry, but they said that person must not have made it as far as I did. I wondered where that person might have turned around.

Although I didn't make it to the stromatolite fossils that day, I really enjoyed the hike, the landscape, and the plants and animals that I saw. It's important to have goals and to push toward them, while not clinging to them and putting yourself into a dangerous situation or preventing yourself from enjoying the other good things the day offers. I felt good about my judgment calls that day and remember it fondly. I wonder how far the young couple got!

*

Time is fathomless, and the Mojave Desert is a perfect example of this. It contains rocks from up to 2.7 billion years ago, over half the age of the Earth. To put this in context, there is less time between us today and the single supercontinents of Pangea and Gondwana than there is time between the formation of these supercontinents and the formation of the Mojave rocks. Today, somewhere in the Mojave's nearly 50,000 square miles lives a ring of creosote bushes estimated to be over 11,700 years old, making it one of the oldest living organisms on Earth. Creosote bushes send out deep roots and suck up so much water that it is sometimes difficult for other things to grow near them. Because of this, creosote seeds don't easily sprout in an area with many creosote bushes, and the plants instead reproduce by sending out new shoots around themselves. As the years have passed, the innermost shoots of this old plant have died off, creating a circular clonal colony plant of genetically identical shoots almost 70 feet in diameter at its widest point. This plant is older than Christ, older than the Buddha, older than the Roman Empire. This plant was already over 7,000 years old when the Pyramids of Giza were being built.

11,700 Year Old Creosote Bush Ring

I was in the Mojave Desert in search of the Burro Schmidt Tunnel. William Henry "Burro" Schmidt lived from 1871 to 1954. He was doing some gold mining in the Mojave around the year 1900 and his burros (donkeys) had to take a treacherous trail around a mountain from where he had built his house to the smelter on the other side. So, he began hand-digging a tunnel through the mountain using a pick, a shovel, and a hammer. A road built in 1920 made the tunnel unnecessary, but Burro

Schmidt continued on. Thirty-eight years after starting, he completed the 0.5 mile long tunnel (not including offshoots) around 1938, although he did have to use dynamite in a few places. A historical placard in the area describes the tunnel as a "monument to determination and perseverance". Although the Burro Schmidt tunnel has a historical marker, it ended up being surprisingly remote.

On the way to the tunnel, I found the entrance to a desert tortoise burrow, with a semicircular tunnel perfectly fitted to the shape of a tortoise shell. Desert tortoises can survive for more than a year without water thanks to the ability to drink up to 40% of their body weight at a single time and to a body that can give off urine waste as a paste rather than liquid urine, saving the urine bladder water as a backup supply. However, desert tortoises empty their bladder as a defense mechanism, which can lead to their death due to dehydration. Because of this, you should never approach or handle a desert tortoise in the wild. Although desert tortoises are elusive (I haven't seen a desert tortoise itself in the wild yet), it's also important to check under your car before driving away in desert tortoise habitat so you don't accidentally crush a tortoise that might be seeking shelter under there.

I arrived at the Burro Schmidt Tunnel and put on my helmet and headlamp. I wasn't too concerned about rockfall in the tunnel, but I'm tall and didn't want to bang my head. Plus, it's especially good to take any precautions you can when solo hiking. I had been out the night before looking for scorpions, a nocturnal creature, but hadn't had any luck. In fact, despite some homeowners complaining of scorpions in their homes, I hadn't ever seen a scorpion in the wild despite searching throughout the southwest, even resorting to leaving my shoes outside my tent after hearing an urban legend about scorpions crawling into your shoes while you sleep. Scorpions have bodies that are photosensitive and help them evade the light and hide more effectively. They're like a giant eyeball with legs, a tail, and claws. As a side effect of this light detection ability, scorpions glow in UV light, and I had purchased a UV flashlight to aid my search, but so far no luck. Perhaps I would see this symbol of the American Southwest (also found throughout the world) in the tunnel during the day.

The Burro Schmidt Tunnel

I started into the tunnel and didn't see any signs of scorpions. However, I soon saw some coyote scat…and then some more coyote scat. I certainly wouldn't want to run into a coyote in this tunnel, much less a mountain lion. The animal would feel cornered and would have few options to escape other than going through me. Running on my part might also trigger a predatory chase in the animal. Hopefully this coyote had passed through the tunnel a long time ago.

I came upon an offshoot to my left with mining cart rails. I explored the offshoot and found it to be very short, so I returned to the main tunnel. Soon, the tunnel curved so that I couldn't see light from outside shining into the entrance anymore and I couldn't yet see light from the exit. I was in complete darkness except for my headlamp and having a great time. Although I've struggled to overcome my fear of heights over the years, I've never had claustrophobia or a fear of being underground or in the lava tubes I've explored in Southern California and Northern Arizona. However, my logical mind has taken note of this lack of emotional fear, and I'm always very careful underground since the emotional alarm bells might not go off. Fear can actually be a helpful trigger.

I get to a branching fork in the tunnel, with the left side extending off into darkness, but I can see light from the exit to my right. I make it to the exit and enjoy the fresh air, but I soon go back into the tunnel to explore the offshoot to the left that I missed. The air quickly changes as a musty, gamey smell hits my nostrils. Could the coyote be back here? Or something worse making a den? I pull out my pepper spray and have it ready in my right hand, while I hold my hiking poles out with my left hand. Hopefully I could make the best of any encounter that might be waiting for me down the tunnel without lasting injury to myself or the animal.

The smell is getting worse, until I arrive at the end of the tunnel and come face to face with a family of mice. Their pellet-like feces and various scraps of detritus cover the ground toward the side of the tunnel. The mice repeatedly freeze in my headlight and then begin to move again when I look away. They repeat this behavior several times as I look back and forth and I feel like I'm turning a set of robot mice off and on.

I exit the tunnel and head from the mountain back to the desert floor, the temperature increasing as I descend.

*

The pronghorn is a beautiful animal with a colorful patterned coat of orange/brown and white. It has no close relatives and is only found in grassland and desert environments of North America. I was hiking the Buenos Aires Wildlife Refuge near the US/Mexico border southwest of Tucson in Arizona looking for the Sonoran pronghorn, which are endangered and have been reintroduced into the refuge in recent years. I was also hoping to see some javelinas, which are pig-like peccaries that are very cute in an ugly sort of way.

On entering the refuge, one of the first animals I saw was a male pyrrhuloxia or desert cardinal. This bird is in the same genus as the more familiar bright red northern cardinal. However, the male pyrrhuloxia is predominantly brown/gray with red highlights and the female pyrrhuloxia is predominantly blue and white with red highlights. Both sexes have a striking color scheme with their stout yellow bills. Their call incorporates the same "pew-pew" sound as the northern cardinal.

I continued my hike and saw on the horizon four deer prancing along together followed by two more deer lagging behind. The fourth deer, last in the first group, decided to stop prancing and took off at top speed, overtaking to first place in the group and spurring the other three deer in the group to chase along. The two straggling deer behind the main group increased their speed a little bit, but seemed not to have the drive of the first group.

The deer made an exciting spectacle, but I initially thought they were pronghorn and became disappointed once I realized they were not. I continued my hike, scanning the terrain all around me from the horizon to the foreground and back again in all directions around me. Up ahead and to the right I saw two figures. I squatted down and moved forward as quickly as I was able. It was an animal mother and her child, but they saw me. I stood up and ran toward them as fast as I could and they took off. In the pursuit, I realized they were more deer rather than pronghorn.

I continued hiking 14 miles and didn't see any pronghorn or javelinas. I gazed at the dramatic Baboquivari Peak, a thick granite monolith rising above the other mountains on the edge of the Tohono O'odham Nation Reservation. I glanced to the north toward the Kitt Peak National Observatory before finally deciding to head out, mentally tired from scanning the landscape. On the drive north, I was stopped at a US Border Patrol checkpoint. I hadn't crossed any borders, but Border Patrol is allowed to set up checkpoints within 100 miles of the border. Only a single agent was staffing the checkpoint. He was 5-10 years younger than me and began his informal interrogation. "Hey man, it's hot out here, huh?" he said. "Oh yeah!" I said. "Are you a US citizen?" he asked. "Yes," I said. "Cool man!" he said, and I was on my way. It's not always that easy.

*

I was spending some time in The Maze district of Canyonlands National Park in Utah. The region is one of the most remote and inaccessible in the continental US and sits east of the Henry Mountains, which was the last mountain range explored and mapped in the lower 48 states. I had made my way to Standing Rock, a spire of mudstone made of tiny clay particles reaching almost 350 feet tall. The sedimentary layers making up the rock are clearly visible. These layers must have formerly covered the entire area before they were eroded away. An erosion-resistant capstone must have protected the layers that now make up Standing Rock.

The rock stands, true to its name, on a canyon ledge looking north across a series of mesas and buttes. What a view! I had camped in the area and had secured my tent with guy lines, which I attached to large rocks rather than using stakes due to the sandstone ground, which is somehow both hard and friable and not ideal for tent stakes. Returning to my campsite one evening, I saw that my tent had nevertheless blown over. I had used heavy enough rocks to secure my tent, but one of the guy lines had broken due to heavy winds sweeping across the canyon. Fortunately, the other guy lines held and my tent didn't get far. A person spending time in a desert environment with high winds will soon end up with sand and other particles in their teeth, under their eyelids, and everywhere else it can reach. You feel the grit when you're talking and inevitably consume some of it. The desert becomes a part of you.

Standing Rock

I walked around Standing Rock and found a pack rat nest, called a midden, nestled on one side. The word "midden" means a trash heap, and this is a good description for the pack rat's home. Sticks, twigs, and debris were mounded up into a dirty partition surrounded by their excrement, providing them a protected space next to the rock.

I continued around the rock and saw a spider web with a black spider a little over an inch in diameter. I walked to the other side of the web and saw the red hourglass on the underside of the spider. I had stumbled upon a black widow, whose venom is 15 times stronger than a rattlesnake's. For some reason, I always thought the red hourglass would be on the spider's back, so I was surprised to see it on the underside. The sp der stayed still as I watched it for a moment, before I moved on.

Despite occasional sand and rats and spiders, the desert feels clean. The heat and aridity lend it a quality of purity compared to many other outdoor environments. Life isn't as abundant as in other biomes, and there seems to be less mess. The pollen that's out here doesn't affect my allergies as much. Maybe doctors were on to something when they noticed dry desert air had a therapeutic effect on tuberculosis patients in the late 1800s and early 1900s. Just don't count on any guaranteed health benefits and become overly complacent. After all, a black widow could unexpectedly be waiting around the corner.

*

The California condor is a critically endangered bird due to habitat loss. In the 1980s, all 27 remaining wild California condors were captured. Breeding programs at the San Diego and Los Angeles zoos have increased their numbers and they have recently been reintroduced into the wild. California condors look similar to turkey vultures, but are much larger with a wider wingspan. Unlike turkey vultures, which have a white zone on the back bottom side of their wings, California condors have a white zone on the bottom front, which is visible as they soar.

I'm hiking north along Bright Angel Creek from the Colorado River toward the North Rim of the Grand Canyon. It's not long after first light and still before sunrise, but I have been hiking since a little after 1 am. It's silent except for the sound of water and a giant, graceful creature glides quietly and low over my head, a California condor.

*

Wolves live and have lived beyond the desert, across North America and Europe, but this experience with a wolf was in what might be considered a desert region. In the continental United States, wolf populations have declined due to loss of habitat, loss of prey such as the American Bison, and extermination campaigns aimed at protecting livestock. However, wolf populations are slowly recovering due to legal protections and reintroduction campaigns.

Officially, wolves are not allowed in the Grand Canyon, however the Grand Canyon is connected to the Blue Range Wolf Recovery Areas to the southeast.

I was hiking on the Arizona Trail in the Kaibab National Forest on the South Rim of the Grand Canyon just before sunrise. I was breathing deeply of the fresh air and ready for the day ahead when I heard the howl of a wolf. It didn't sound at all like the howls children make when imitating wolves, it was more complex than that with a wild quality and a guttural ending. Being alone, the sounds sent chills up my spine...and brought a smile to my face.

*

The city of Palm Springs, California and the surrounding Coachella Valley brings to mind mid-century modern architecture, resorts, golf courses, Marilyn Monroe, and Frank Sinatra. But, for me, it also brings to mind sandstorms and the Desert Riders. The Desert Riders are a social club that started in the 1930s out of a shared love of horses and horseback riding. However, club activities soon expanded to include trail creation, and many of these trails are still in use today as lasting contributions to the community. Two of my favorites are the Art Smith Trail and the Boo Hoff Trail.

Trail creation and building are more complex than you might imagine. It's not just about clearing a straight path from one place to another. Planners have to take into account the contours of the land, the flow of water, and the effects of erosion. Trail camber and large rocks will affect the course of water. Builders may need to reinforce certain areas with rock walls or other supports and the trail itself may have multiple layers of different gravel and rocks underneath the visible dirt on the surface, in order to manage drainage. Trails need to lead to points of interest where people want to go in order to minimize "use trails" being created due to people going off trail and wearing a path.

But, the trails we use today are not all modern creations. Many are adaptations of ancient trails that Native Americans or even animals first created and used, and this was the case with many of the Desert Riders' trails. In very rough terrain, there may only be a single "best path" through, so humans might take the same path as animals or animals might follow a trail created by humans. No trail is in isolation and many change dynamically over the decades and centuries.

I like horses and horse people. However, there are practical problems with hikers and horses sharing the same trail, the chief one being horse excrement. Horses let loose whenever they feel like it and in trails that get a lot of use by horses, their waste seems to completely cover the path. This is also a problem on the corridor trails of the Grand Canyon, where mules carry loads in and out of the canyon several times a day. Decades of mule feces have turned to dust that forms a kind of topsoil. Maybe I'm missing something, but I don't understand why the mules don't have bags hanging under them to catch their waste. It's not just a matter of keeping the trails clean. Phosphorus from waste can make its way into water sources and cause algal blooms which threaten other life. This is why high-use trails, such as the Grand Canyon corridor trails, have rest houses with pit toilets for humans. The waste needs to be contained to prevent environmental damage.

Back to the Palm Springs area, I was once hiking the Boo Hoff Trail as my first hike of the season in very hot temperatures. I was enjoying the landscape when a hummingbird flew up to me and stayed around long enough for me to get a photo. Its wings were a blur to my eyes, but the photo captures them in freeze frame. Hummingbird wings flap up to 80 beats per minute and they have incredible maneuverability.

Hummingbird

I continued my hike that day and soon saw a large tamarisk or salt cedar tree. The needle-like leaves of a tamarisk look similar to juniper leaves to me, but the tamarisk also produces large clusters of pink/purple flowers on fingered strands. It's a beautiful plant, but it's also an invasive species that threatens native species by outcompeting them. The tamarisk is excellent at pulling water from drying soil, leaving little water for other plants, and it concentrates salt on the outside of its leaves. When these leaves fall off, they create a layer of topsoil with higher salinity, which can inhibit the germination of other plants until the salt is washed off by rainwater or flooding.

I finished up my hike by walking through a developed area where construction workers were working in the heat. Of all the physically difficult jobs in the world, being a construction worker in the desert must be near the top and these people have my respect. As I walked past the site, one of the workers called out to me, "Hey man, how far are you going?" The implied ending to the question was, "in this heat". "About twelve and a half miles," I replied. "DAY-UM!" the workers exploded. Their reactions made me smile, but seriously, day-um, those workers were the tough ones.

*

Charles Debrille Poston lived from 1825 to 1902 and is known as the "Father of Arizona". He was quite an eclectic character! Poston was the managing supervisor of a mine in Tubac, Arizona, which was at that time part of the territory of New Mexico. He seems to have been a very welcoming person, and employed Mexicans, escaped black slaves, Native Americans, and white settlers. He was soon printing his own money and officiating over marriages, divorces, and the baptism of children. A vicar from Santa Fe questioned the validity of these marriages, but soon sanctified the unions after a donation was made to the vicar and Poston promised to refrain from these ceremonies in the future. When the Civil War started, Union troops were pulled out of the area, leading to an increase in hostilities with Apaches, and Poston and his employees fled the territory, escaping with their lives.

Poston made a series of trips between Washington, DC and Arizona over the coming years, traveling by ship through the Panama Canal to San Francisco, and then continuing over land to Arizona from there. He eventually convinced President Abraham Lincoln and Congress to split the New Mexico territory, creating a separate Arizona territory. New Mexico was originally going to be in the north, since Santa Fe was in the north, and Arizona was going to be in the south, since Tucson was in the south (this was before Phoenix was established and the state capital was transferred between Tucson, Prescott, and Phoenix before finally settling at Phoenix). However, officials in Santa Fe wanted New Mexico to include fertile lands in the south near the Pecos River, so an east-west split was agreed upon.

Poston traveled the world in a time when doing so was much more difficult than today. He eventually converted to Zoroastrianism and wanted to build a temple on top of a butte near Florence, Arizona. He even petitioned the Shah of Iran for funding, but the temple was not to be. After Poston died, he was buried in Phoenix, but his remains were later moved to the top of the same butte where he wanted to build his temple, and a stone pyramid honoring him marks the site today.

Zoroastrian practice includes the worship of the sun god Mithra. I was hiking Poston Butte before dawn looking for javelinas in the brush at the base of the mountain. I was near the summit as the sun rose, and at that moment I heard several calls from the peak and saw a man facing the sun in joy. I don't know if this man was a Zoroastrian or not, but I'm sure Poston would have approved. I gave the man his space and greeted him when he descended, before spending some time with the "Father of Arizona".

Although I have heard stories of large squadrons of javelinas wandering through suburbs and supermarket parking lots in Phoenix at twilight, they have always been evasive to me. My search for javelinas had been unsuccessful that day and on many other days in the past. I wanted to see them in person, so I headed to the Phoenix Zoo.

The Phoenix Zoo is located in Papago Park, which contains the grave of Arizona's first governor, George W. P. Hunt, adorned with a pyramid memorial. Arizona historical figures must really like pyramid memorials! Papago Park was used as a camp for prisoners of war during World War II. German U-boat submariners were sent to this desert environment, so different from the waters in which they had fought. Twenty-five of these submariners would escape by digging a tunnel through what was thought to be impenetrable earth, leading to one of the largest manhunts in US history. However, the submariners were ill-equipped to survive in the desert environment and soon were captured or turned themselves in. Some of the prisoners had seen the Salt River on a map and had managed to build a collapsible raft before the escape, which they hoped would carry them down the Salt River and eventually to the Gulf of California via the Gila River and the Colorado River. However, the prisoners found the Salt River was dry, and quickly abandoned their plan.

The Phoenix Zoo was experiencing triple-digit Fahrenheit temperatures the day of my visit, and had limited opening hours of 7 am-11 am. I frequently visited the water bottle refilling stations and was happy not to have to carry gallons of water on my back. I was very pleased with the exhibits on local wildlife, however in some of the exhibits their inhabitants were nowhere to be seen. This was the case with the scorpion area. Even in a zoo, the scorpions had evaded me! I enjoyed seeing desert creatures such as burrowing owls and desert tortoises. Finally, I spent a good amount of time at the javelina exhibit. Most of the javelinas were lying in the shade, but a few of them were moving around and I was able to enjoy them from behind a barrier without worrying about one of them charging at me.

Javelinas

*

I was heading into the deep desert in hopes of finally finding a scorpion with my UV light. It was difficult to say for sure, but if I found a scorpion on this trip, it still might be the most effort I've spent on searching for an animal per gram of animal body weight. Yes, the scorpion is an animal, an arachnid belonging to the kingdom Animalia.

I made it to a flat, low area surrounded by mountains on the far horizon, an area that had almost no light from artificial sources. It was past astronomical twilight and the night sky was as dark as it would get. The night was hot, which was a good thing, since scorpions are most active in the heat. I looked up and my jaw dropped as I saw the Milky Way galaxy stretching across the sky. But, the Milky Way wasn't an object out there. The Earth is in the Milky Way, a part of it. I was on a rock moving through inconceivably vast space and looking out into it. I stared at a spot in the sky and saw faint points of light start to appear where I didn't see them before as my eyes adjusted. This was a place where it was dark enough that the human eye could look as deeply into space and time as it is able. The constellations all had many more points of light than we ordinarily see. I felt small, but I also felt oriented in space and time, like I belonged right where I was. I was bathed in awe, with a touch of existential dread.

My dread looking into the universe came from an understanding of my own mortality, but there was also a flip side to this dread, which was a profound peace and a desire to do what I could of meaning for myself and others, to make whatever loving imprint I was able to in my time. Working through my fear of heights in the past brought forth a different type of dread. I was afraid of slipping and falling, but I was also afraid of throwing myself into the abyss. My ultimate freedom was highlighted, but so were the conflicting tendencies within me. I was capable of heroism and of helplessness, and while I could develop my skills and knowledge, I was also fallible. Working through my inner world when confronted with heights gave me the courage to look into the vast universe. My fear of heights is still there, but I relate to it differently.

A meteorite shot across the sky and down toward the horizon, the Earth's atmosphere continually protecting us from bombardment. You can see meteorites more frequently than you might think if you're in the habit of looking up when you're outside in the evening, and sightings become even more frequent if you spend time in dark, remote locations. Maybe my mind plays a trick on me, but when meteorites are low enough, you can hear an audible noise as they burn and you can see the burning remnants linger for a moment in the path where the meteorite passed.

I saw a bright satellite pass by. Although we're on a part of the Earth facing away from the sun during the night, satellites may still be able to catch the sun's rays and reflect them toward Earth. The luminous satellite will move at a steady pace across the night sky, and you can sometimes see the fading light as it passes into the edge of the Earth's shadow, the Earth's penumbra, in space. These "satellite flares" normally happen earlier in the evening, so seeing one after astronomical twilight was special.

I started walking through the desert, shining my UV light around, looking on the desert floor and on and under the cacti and other plants. No scorpions were immediately visible, and there was a brief feeling that this wasn't going to be a fruitful search, especially since I had just come from an unsuccessful scorpion search in a different location the night before. However, I realized I couldn't expect scorpions to pop out of nowhere on command, so I continued my search. I saw what I thought was a scrap of paper or trash on the ground glowing brightly (as I'd seen before), but when I got closer it was a small scorpion! "Oh, wow," I gasped in all sincerity, as I've been known to do in other encounters with nature. The little scorpion stayed put for a bit, and I tried not to overexpose it to UV light in case this might cause a harmful effect. I also viewed it with the light of my headlamp to see the natural colors of the scorpion. The scorpion scurried toward a bush, where it grabbed one of the many small bugs hovering around in its claws.

I continued my search and soon saw a large scorpion. Its details were amazingly visible. Finally, on my way back, I saw a third scorpion of medium size. Three scorpions in one night, what finds! I later looked up my finds and identified them as dune scorpions, although I wasn't sure about the small one. The scorpions were all pretty friendly, all things considered. They were all on the ground and didn't scurry away much or jump or make threatening gestures with their claws or tail. I wondered if I was as new to them as they were to me or if they had seen humans with headlamps and UV lights before. My search had paid off!

Dune Scorpion

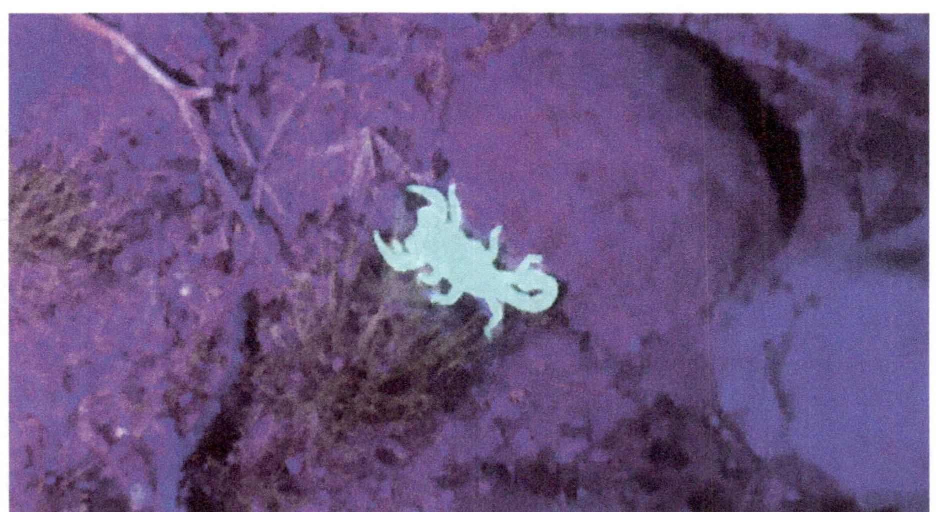

Glowing Dune Scorpion in UV Light

*

I was hiking in a low-lying area of the Colorado Desert in Southern California, part of the larger Sonoran Desert. For the past 6 million years, the Gulf of California has advanced inland and retreated again in cycles across this area as tectonic plates have moved and shifted. In the past 2.5 million years, Lake Cahuilla has cyclically formed and disappeared in the region. Today, the Salton Sea is located a little over 25 miles away from here as measured by a straight line on a map.

The area is dry and barren, there isn't even much vegetation. Caves carved out of sandstone formations by the wind sit on cliff ledges. It's difficult to imagine this area being covered by a sea, ocean, or lake, however the legacy of water is visible in the fossils of marine life left behind and the slot canyons carved by it more recently.

I was hiking through a canyon and looking at the canyon walls. What first appeared to be rough rock revealed itself to be thousands of fossilized seashells as I got closer. I absorbed all the details of what was in front of me and imagined how many shells must have been inside of the rock. These shells must have fallen to the bottom of a sea where they formed shell reefs and were fossilized.

Thousands of Fossilized Seashells

The canyon narrowed and I continued into a dry slot canyon. Part of the slot canyon floor had large potholes or depressions which I had to either edge my way around, climb down into and back out of, or if they were small enough, step over to cross. Near the far side of the slot canyon, I found several fossils of large sand dollars embedded in the rock before I emerged into a vista of colorful mountains, painted by minerals deposited by the ancient ebbing and flowing waters.

Sand Dollar Fossils

Thirty-five miles north of here, high-quality calcite was mined during World War II for making aircraft bomb sights. Optical grade calcium carbonate calcite crystals performed well for this application until a synthetic replacement was created. Calcite comes from limestone, which is formed from the shells of dead marine life. Large volumes of marine life must have lived and died here to be able to provide the raw materials extracted by this mining operation.

The fact that a hot, dry, barren desert has marine fossils from millions of years ago in such quantities shows how much the Earth, climate, and landscape change over time. Poets may write of the seeming permanence of features like mountains and deserts, but landscapes are always and inexorably in flux.

<u>Mountains</u>

I was hiking along a chaparral trail through the mountains, trying to get a break from everything going on in the world. The word "chaparral" comes from the Spanish "chaparro", meaning "place of the scrub oak". It's a scrubland biome where bushes dominate, sort of halfway between grassland and a forest. It was still early in the COVID-19 pandemic, but trails were reopening for the first time since initially being closed to the public following the pandemic outbreak. Apparently I wasn't the only one enjoying a fresh change of scenery. Across a valley, I saw another hiker. He yelled to me, "No COVID out here!" I pumped my arms in the air and returned a yell of affirmation. The fact that a valley separated us and that neither one of us attempted to get any closer to the other despite both of us surely facing social isolation showed that we were deluding ourselves to a degree. Nothing about this scrubland was COVID resistant other than the isolation. Nevertheless, it felt good to be out again.

As I continued down the trail, I heard a high-frequency rattle from the bushes to my right. I immediately knew this was a rattlesnake, but it took my eyes a moment to see the source of the sound, a western diamondback rattlesnake. Western diamondback rattlesnake venom damages the nervous system, muscles, heart, and blood cells, so I applied the 6 foot social distancing rule I was so familiar with to this snake. The trail was more narrow than this, and for a moment, I considered whether I should pass. However, I was able to work my way into the bushes on the opposite side of the trail and slightly down the mountainside to reach the 6 foot threshold. I quickly went past the snake, staying alert, and continued safely on my way. Healthcare workers were dealing with enough as it was, and I didn't need to be a further burden on them for non-COVID reasons.

*

I've seen signs posted to watch out for mountain lions on trails, but had never seen mountain lions themselves. This animal seemed to me like the biggest ghost of the wilderness out there, and looking for them felt like searching for bigfoot.

One day I asked myself what I would do if seeing a mountain lion, also known as a puma, cougar, panther, or catamount, was my most important goal. If I couldn't decide which name to call them, what hope would I ever have of seeing one? My dad was a veterinarian and growing up, I remember a "cougar" from a local pet shop would sometimes receive care from him (I somehow prefer the term "mountain lion"). I loved looking at that mountain lion, but I wanted to see one in the wild. If that were really my goal, maybe I would hike with raw meat hanging from my pack or camp out in front of a pile of steaks. No, that wouldn't work, mountain lions rarely scavenge and prefer to kill their own food.

I remembered nature photographers in wildlife documentaries spend weeks sitting in the wilderness hidden by photography blinds. They have to stay alert waiting for the perfect shot. I've also seen motion-activated cameras placed in the wilderness for extended periods of time, to later be retrieved and their footage used in documentaries. However, I wasn't sure what that would involve.

I knew that mountain lions normally stay away from humans unless they are desperate for food or have an unexpected encounter with us. I had a healthy respect for mountain lions, but didn't fear them. Nevertheless, preparations and precautions are necessary. I often carry pepper spray with mountain lions in mind, among other animals and humans. If stalked or approached by a persistent mountain lion, I'd make myself as large as I could, make noise and let it hear my human words, and perhaps throw rocks toward it if I could pick some up without bending over (a position of prey). I have a feeling my trekking poles would also be helpful.

When old enough, young males disperse from their birth family to establish a territory with multiple females. Due to habitat loss and fragmentation, this male dispersal sometimes results in encounters with humans. Sometimes ranches are built in mountain lion migration corridors and a cycle develops where livestock are killed, a predation permit is issued for the lion, the lion is killed, and then there's calm until the next mountain lion comes along and more livestock are killed. It seems measures such as livestock pens with roofs or putting the livestock in barns for the night would be better for the ranchers and better for the mountain lions.

Mountain lions have a stealth ambush hunting strategy rather than chasing down prey. This is probably how the bighorn from earlier in this book was killed at the spring. Mountain lions like to wait high on cliffs or in trees or in border regions between two different types of landscape, such as forest and grasslands and then pounce on prey when they pass.

Mountain lions are distributed throughout North and South America, but in the US, they are mainly found west of the Rocky Mountains, although their historical range extended to the East Coast. Nevertheless, mountain lions have been resilient in the face of threats from humans and the wider natural world.

The Florida panther is one remnant of the mountain lion's East Coast presence. They're an "at risk" population, and some renowned photographs taken from motion-activated trail cameras have appeared in National Geographic Magazine, accompanied by the release of a documentary film.

I decided that motion-activated trail cameras with LED lights that turn on when motion is detected at night might be the best way to document footage of a mountain lion for myself and easier than seeing one in person in the wild. I bought two cameras along with enough batteries to leave both in the wilderness for a month and a 32 GB SD card for each to store the footage. The cameras were camouflaged and sealed against water. Mountain lions are sometimes captured by wildlife management agencies and fitted with radio collars before being released again. I found some radio collar data online, noted the most densely populated areas, and decided where to place my cameras.

I set out into the mountains in late December hiking along the Pacific Crest Trail before departing on another route. I carefully placed each camera and hiked back. On my hike out, I met a woman hiking along the trail and cleaning things up. She was a "trail angel" who lived along the PCT and welcomed long-distance hikers to stay on her property when they would seasonally pass through en masse in the springtime. She would provide them with food and water and seemed like a really kind person. I enjoyed talking with her and I read some of her poetry, which she had written for the new year. She introduced me to a species of bush in the area called ribbonwood or red shank. Unfortunately, I heard recently that she decided to retire from her volunteer role as a trail angel and relocate to Montana after repeated thefts of her property, not from hikers, but from locals in the area. I wish her all the best and thank her for her contributions to the community. I'm grateful I was able to find a way to contact her directly to express my wishes and thanks in person.

I returned a month later to retrieve my cameras. Once they were in my pack, I felt so pleased, but when I got home and looked at the footage I only saw one video of a bird flying by and another of a hiker passing by and sticking out their tongue at the camera. At least the hiker didn't take the camera. I guess the camouflage on the cameras isn't perfect!

*

I'm driving through the mountains of Utah. This terrain is so high that they sell 85 octane gasoline as standard unleaded. Most standard unleaded gasoline is 87 octane, and that's the minimum that most manufacturers recommend. The higher the octane, the more resistant the gasoline is to exploding due to heat and pressure before it gets to the combustion chamber, which could damage the engine. At higher altitudes, there is less atmospheric pressure, and you can get away with a lower octane. However, you can run into trouble if you descend from altitude with 85 octane in your tank and newer cars with their electronic sensors and software programming don't handle 85 octane well, either. 85 octane is cheaper than 87 octane, but I avoid it.

Technical thoughts like these are far from my mind, however, as I maneuver my vehicle through each beautiful curve of the mountainside. This is driving as it's meant to be, in the wide open and limited only by the terrain, the vehicle, and your combined abilities, not driving 20 mph on a straight state highway through a small town with roads so wide Brigham Young could have designed them (those who have visited Salt Lake City know what I'm talking about), pretending like this is the only safe and reasonable speed for the environment. With as much traveling as I do, however, I always obey those 20 mph signs and watch for children chasing balls into the street. If I were a parent in a town like that and my children were playing ball next to the state highway, I'd be worried that drivers' eyes were on their speedometers rather than on the road.

I go over a crest in the road and see a large bird and two smaller birds in flight fighting to my left. The larger bird has dark feathers which flare out on the ends of the wings like fingers, with white feathers on the head and tail, and a yellow beak and talons. It's a bald eagle.

*

I am descending from Quandary Peak in Colorado, my first 14er. A solid 35 mph wind has been blowing throughout the day and it has increased to 40mph. I've reached the maximum wind speed limit I allow myself. I'm above the treeline, but quickly approaching it. Before I get there, I see a mountain goat in the distance. I watch it for a moment before it slips out of view, following the curve of the mountain away from me.

The mountain goat, Oreamnos americanus, is the only living species of its genus. With a scientific name like that, you know it's an iconic American animal. Iconic or not, it lives in a narrow range, and I'm happy to have seen its short horns and white scruff.

*

Although they're often referred to as "buffalo", the American bison is not a buffalo at all. These large animals once roamed the plains in vast herds, but were nearly driven to extinction by hunting, intentional slaughter, and disease from commercial cattle. Many Native American tribes hunted bison, sometimes killing them in large numbers by driving herds off cliffs. However, settlers began killing the bison in even greater numbers, often for sport, taking a souvenir body part and leaving the rest of the animal to rot. As the railroad stretched across the country, tourists would shoot bison from the train cars as they would go by. The federal government actively encouraged the slaughter of bison in order to remove the Native Americans' main food source and force them into reservations. Their only other alternative was to remain on the land and starve.

Although the bison is an animal of the plains and forest, my experience with them came on a mountainous island. Santa Catalina Island in the Channel Islands off the coast of California is an interesting place. A short boat ride from the mainland, tourists come to the island to enjoy the water and the scenery, scuba diving, snorkeling, parasailing, fishing, hiking, and more. The island has a storied history including smuggling and searches for gold. Chewing gum magnate William Wrigley, Jr. played a large role in developing the tourist potential of the island, and the Chicago Cubs even trained there. When Wrigley died, he was buried near his home on Catalina Island, but his body was later moved to the mainland.

I took an ATV tour of the island as a passenger, this time leaving the driving to a professional who kept up the needed momentum to surmount steep slopes and maneuvered the vehicle through tight turns like it was a slot car. It was lovely to see the blue sky meet the blue ocean.

In the 1920s, bison were brought to Catalina Island for the filming of a silent movie and have remained there ever since. I came upon a number of the bison on my ATV tour and when we stopped, I got off the ATV and watched them munching away on vegetation and shooing flies with their tails.

American Bison

*

It was early June and I had decided on a new location to place my trail cameras to hopefully record a mountain lion, the Santa Ana Mountains. I had read that this area had a high mountain lion population, and male lions would disperse from here to other sites in Southern California. I bought fresh batteries for the cameras and was ready to go.

The hike to place my cameras wasn't fun, so much so that I considered whether I wanted to turn back so I didn't have to do the hike a second time to retrieve them. The first part of the hike was a bumpy paved road, which I generally try to avoid hiking on. I prefer to have my feet on the earth, which is softer and can take you to more secluded locations. This road had multiple areas where a stream had flooded over it, so I had to choose to ford the stream or toss out stepping stones and cross while stabilizing myself with trekking poles. I had experience crossing streams, and I preferred the stepping stone approach, but doing it over pavement felt strange.

I pressed on after the paved section to a section of dirt road with such a high volume of traffic that the dirt had turned to dust, with particles the size of powdered sugar. I probably had 70 vehicles pass me that day, and each one kicked up a huge cloud of dust. My neck gaiter was very helpful in covering my nose and mouth. The overall feel was like hiking on a dusty, flooded highway.

Finally, I turned off the dirt road and onto a drainage path, and I started to enjoy the scenery. A Coulter pine with spiky ten pound pine cones as big as your head was growing to the side of my path. A mountain chickadee calmed me with a call of three high tones followed by two low tones. Unfortunately, there were lots of insects bothering me, but I was able to get a close look at an insect whose name had been puzzling me on recent adventures and identify it as a bee fly. They look just like a mix between a bee and a fly and have interesting delta wings.

The drainage path took me to two spots where I dropped off my cameras. One camera was at an elevation of 4,257 feet and the other at an elevation of 4,532 feet, about 0.4 miles apart. There was lots of scat from various animals in the area, including mountain lion scat, so I felt confident this was a travel corridor for animals through the mountains. One of the cameras was next to a scent scrape. Mountain lions use their back legs to slowly scrape a path in the dirt, leaving a mound of dirt piled up on one side. They'll sometimes urinate or defecate on this mound in order to leave their scent. However, I wasn't completely sure that this scrape was from a mountain lion, it might have been created by a coyote or a fox. All I could do now was wait for a month.

*

While I waited to pick up my cameras, I had mountain lions on my mind. An unexpected change in my schedule opened up an opportunity for me to look for the remains of a Native American mountain lion shrine that I had heard about, which featured two stone mountain lion statues carved from boulders. The exact location of many Native American artifacts is not publicly disclosed in order to protect them from vandalism or theft. There seems to be even more secrecy when the artifacts are within an hour or so of a city (which could attract increased traffic if people knew exactly where they were) or when the site is still being used for ceremonial purposes, both of which were the case for the shrine. Nevertheless, many artifacts are on public land where the public is allowed to be. I would have to hope that I had picked up enough clues from online images and articles to have planned my hike in the right general location, and scan the terrain as I had done looking for pronghorn and javelinas in the wildlife refuge earlier.

I started my hike about an hour outside of Santa Fe, New Mexico and was really enjoying myself and the landscape. The landscape seemed like classic New Mexico to me, and was quite varied. I had just finished descending into and ascending out of a canyon when I noticed flakes of stone at my feet. Perhaps Native Americans had done stonework in the area. I continued and soon saw small pottery shards. I followed them, as if they were a trail, and they led off to my left. Before I knew it, I had come upon the remains of an unexcavated Native American pueblo village, which wasn't on my radar at all!

Unexcavated Native American Pueblo Village

I never thought I'd find myself in a place like this and my jaw dropped. Surprise, joy, and reverence filled my being. I spent some time exploring, but treading very lightly. There were beautiful painted pottery shards and I tried to imagine what life must have been like living in the village. I think I would have enjoyed it.

Pottery Shard

I found the remains of a circular underground kiva, where ceremonies were performed, but no sign of the mountain lion shrine. Traditional Navajo Nation beliefs say the Diné (the people) emerged into this world from underground. Perhaps the people in this village held a similar belief. Either way, the underground kiva must have been a sacred place.

With a happy heart, I continued my hike looking for the shrine. I passed a clearing on my left where a woman was standing, and she had left her bag near where I was passing. A bag or trekking poles left near a trail or path can be a request for privacy, particularly if their owner is relieving themselves off-trail. In this case, I thought the woman might have been camping in the clearing, and I didn't want to disturb her. As I passed, she started walking in my general direction and I almost said hello and asked if she had seen anything interesting; I almost shared my experience. However, I wasn't quite ready to enter back into the world of modern humans after my time in the village and she didn't say anything either.

I completed my hike without finding the mountain lion shrine, despite finding actual mountain lion scat in the area and some elk bones scattered and probably killed by coyotes. It must have been a good area for a shrine, so close to the real thing, but it seemed anything related to mountain lions was an imperceptible ghost to me.

Looking at satellite images of the area, I later realized that the woman I had seen on my hike was standing inside the mountain lion shrine. There were rocks arranged in a circle around her, but I thought it was just an area cleared for camping. There were two boulders on the inside of the circle, which must have been the carved lions, but they were apparently too eroded for me to recognize from where I was passing by. I was so, so close.

Still wanting to see mountain lions carved from stone, I bought a beautiful small mountain lion stone statue carved by a Zuni artisan. This statue was intended for sale, but traditionally would have been a kind of talisman intended to provide protection and convey identity. The Zuni people live in New Mexico, but trace their spiritual origin to the junction of the Little Colorado River and the Colorado River, where the Grand Canyon and Marble Canyon meet. My girlfriend has been to this junction and has shown me photographs of blue water mixing with the brown sediment being transported by the Colorado River.

In 2022, the Federal Energy Regulatory Commission canceled two preliminary permits for dams on the Little Colorado River near the junction with the Colorado River. As of July 2023, a third project to dam the nearby Big Canyon is pending. This isn't the first time dams have been planned in the area, with a Marble Canyon dam being proposed and defeated in the 1960s. I understand the essential need for water and energy in society, but I can't imagine building a dam in or right next to a World Heritage Site like the Grand Canyon.

A week later when I was cleaning, I accidentally knocked the mountain lion statue off a shelf and the tail broke off. Had the talisman turned into a bad omen for my trail cameras? Fortunately, I was able to glue the tail back on with super glue. The Japanese art of kintsugi repairs broken objects using precious metals such as gold. The break becomes part of the history of the object rather than something to hide. Perhaps I could still piece together my search for a mountain lion. I'm still glad I used superglue rather than gold, however. You can't even see a crack on the statue.

*

I was at a petroglyph site on the outskirts of Albuquerque, New Mexico. Long ago, a mountain stood at this site. About 200,000 years ago, volcanic eruptions sent out lava flows, which wrapped around the mountain and hardened. The mountain eventually eroded away, but the erosion-resistant lava remained in a crescent ridge around the now-vanished mountain. Around 550 years ago, petroglyphs were carved into the rocks making up this ridge by pecking or scraping away the dark surface of these volcanic rocks to reveal the lighter-colored rock underneath.

After some searching, I found the petroglyph of a macaw that I had in mind. The four lines making up its tail feather were reminiscent of the Zia sun symbol. Macaws aren't native to this region, so I was curious why the bird had been carved into the volcanic rock. Perhaps the climate was different long ago, and the macaws lived further north at that time? No, macaws never got farther north than Central America, and predominantly live in South America today. I took some photos of the area, and went on my way, pondering the mystery.

Macaw Petroglyph

It wasn't until I was looking at one of my photos of the macaw petroglyph later that I realized what I thought were indecipherable scratches to the lower left of the main bird, was actually a representation of a bird in a cage! The bird in the cage is facing to the right and leaving forward with its wings above its body. Perhaps this petroglyph is evidence of a macaw trade with Central and South America. I imagine the colorful feathers of the macaw would have been valuable for decoration and perhaps ceremony.

Other types of parrots in the macaw's Psittacidae family have made an appearance in the American Southwest outside of their normal range. Although their origins are a mystery, several species of parrots have taken up residence in San Diego, California. They were probably intentionally or accidentally released on a number of different occasions, and given San Diego's proximity to the border, may have been brought to the area through the black market pet trade. I've seen the parrots in the palm trees of several beachside communities there and whenever they show up, they're quite a surprise. Although the desert fan palm is native to desert regions of San Diego County, most of the decorative palm trees seen in the urban and residential landscaping of Southern California are non-native species. There, parrots survive off food from non-native fruiting and flowering palm trees and other non-native trees, and the trees also serve as shelters for the birds. Many of these parrot species are doing better in San Diego than in their native ranges and are now considered naturalized.

*

When I went to pick up my trail cameras, I set off from the trailhead just before sunrise in hopes of encountering less traffic on the dusty dirt road. My strategy worked, and made for a much more pleasant hike than the first time. I was pleased to recover both of my cameras and grateful no person or animal had stolen or damaged them.

The paved section was still flooded in parts, but not as much as the first time. When I got back to it on the way out, I saw a woman looking through binoculars standing next to her SUV, which was pulled over on the side of the pavement. I recognized her from when I first placed my cameras. She said hello and asked if I just went to the end of the paved section. I told her I had gone much farther and was picking up some trail cameras, hopefully to capture footage of a mountain lion. I should have been more discreet. "Who are you to be placing cameras out here?" she asked.

"Who am I, indeed?" I think.

The concept of identity can cause problems.

"After all, I don't have a degree in biology or anthropology or paleontology or geomorphology. Did I really deserve to be out here? Why am I always pushing the limit? Why can't I just be content with things as they are and fall in line with expectations."

Questions of identity, doubt, and conventional thinking follow each other like links on a chain.

"And what am I doing trying to understand and connect with other cultures? We're constrained and formed by genetics and society. I can never truly know what it's like to be from another culture, because my background and culture are different. I can't relate to others. We should stick to our own communities, our safe spaces. Sometimes justice even requires it, doesn't it?"

Maybe. Or maybe there's a raw awareness behind our cultural and genetic conditioning, not bound by convention. Perhaps there is a shared humanity that lets us understand and respect one another as individuals and have compassion for others. Maybe the links of identity, doubt, and convention form a chain that is tying us down. What would it take to break free?

I snap out of my philosophical daydream. The question remains unanswered, "Who are you?" "I'm just a citizen," I say. "Are you with the county? Are you posting GPS coordinates of mountain lion sightings online?" "No," I say, "At the moment, I don't even use social media."

The woman calms down and explains that a male mountain lion with mange on his face has been spotted in the area. He's acting abnormally and was recently "scratching on a female's door". I don't see anything wrong with that at first, after all, how is a mountain lion bachelor supposed to get a date if he can't go knocking on some female lion's door. However, this woman was speaking like a biologist. What she meant to say was that the lion was scratching on a woman's door in the nearby town. She's clearly concerned that the county is putting out cameras in hopes of finding this lion and killing it.

The woman tells me about conservation work she's doing with a foundation. She's currently out counting nests. She's outside almost every day, and after fifty years in the field has seen five mountain lions. That's a higher number than many professionals attempting to study lions, but it's over fifty years of almost daily effort! These lions are indeed elusive. We finish our conversation, I thank her for her conservation work, and I go on my way.

When I arrive home, I start going through the footage on the first camera and am pleased to see several videos of a gray fox, a bobcat (I can see the white behind its ears), and some deer.

They are beautiful scenes with varied light conditions throughout the day and night. Then, I see the unmistakable curve of the tail of a mountain lion close to the cameras, illuminated by my camera's LEDs against the night.

Mountain Lion Hindquarters and Tail

I slap my hands together, yell out a "yeah!", and disturb the neighbors. I've got it, I could be satisfied with this. The footage of the other animals is great, too. A fox is rubbing the scent gland under its head on the ground to mark its territory, and a deer is moving its ears around, alert for predators. It has good reason to be on the lookout.

I start to go through the footage on the second camera and I see more deer, before finally seeing the body and face of a mountain lion. I can't believe my luck, there it is! The mountain lions from both cameras appeared on the same night, so I think they are the same animal. It doesn't appear to have mange. I also have a clear view of the animal's neck and there is no radio collar. This mountain lion hasn't been captured and tagged by wildlife management agencies. It's unknown to them…it's completely wild.

Mountain Lion

I find it interesting that the deer appeared to be looking directly at the camera at night, perhaps because of the motion-activated lights. However, the mountain lion didn't seem disturbed by the light at all. After a month of monitoring on two cameras, I have 2 minutes and 53 seconds of total footage, and it was worth it.

*

During the California Gold Rush, miners relied on a wild plant in the region as a source of vitamin C to avoid scurvy. Today we know this plant as miner's lettuce. I had been keeping an eye out for miner's lettuce for ten years, but it wasn't until I saw a patch of it growing wild during a hike with my girlfriend in the mountains of Southern California that I was able to definitely see it for myself. We each sampled a leaf and found it to have a taste like spinach, but sweeter and with more texture and crunch. We were so happy to finally find this plant, which played such an important role in California history. Once I had seen these plants, I began to recognize miner's lettuce on many more trails. The plants that we had first recognized had unusually large leaves, which made them stand out, but the plant normally grows to a smaller size. I just needed an oversized example to help me recognize miner's lettuce in the future.

My girlfriend and I were on another hike in the mountains and the smell of white sage was in the air. We soon came upon some wild blackberries and sampled a few after positively identifying them. On the way back, we ran into some free range cattle, which were allowed to graze in the area in exchange for the ranchers paying a fee to the land management agency. These cattle didn't have horns and you wouldn't expect a cow to be threatening. However, these cattle were large animals and there were so many of them that they put us on our guard. I'd had other encounters with cattle while hiking and driving across free range pastureland before and had also stayed alert on those occasions. These animals weren't moving unless they wanted to and who knew what they would do if one panicked. We approached them speaking aloud calmly to avoid surprises and several of the cattle glared in our direction, either unhappy or indifferent. One of them startled for a moment and jumped away, but that was the extent of the disturbance. We passed by these creatures and went on our way.

Solo hiking is great in that it provides an opportunity to connect with yourself, become more independent, pursue the things that interest you, and meet others along the way. It even allows you to be creative and develop your own ways of doing things. The pressure is off and you can focus more easily on the environment around you. Solo hikers may also be more likely to see animals since a single hiker likely makes less noise than two or more people and there are fewer humans for the animals to sense and run away or hide.

However, hiking with others also has its advantages. It allows you to spend quality time with those close to you, it provides opportunities to learn from others with different skill sets or more experience, it's a great way to get acquainted with new people, it provides a safety net in case you get into trouble, and you can connect with a community. Joy shared is joy multiplied, and that's particularly true when in nature together. Hiking with friends and loved ones creates shared memories, allows you to work on overcoming obstacles together and improving communication, and creates a culture in your relationship that values simple, healthy, outdoor time.

Having a healthy sense of self-confidence is important for being able to connect with others in healthy ways, and hiking solo or with others is a great way to develop that self-confidence. A full life involves both time alone and time with others.

It always feels so good to spend time with my girlfriend in nature, and foraging together created memories I'll cherish. Being outside together allows us to connect with each other directly without external influence and support each other along the way. I always look forward to our next adventure together!

Plains

I was spending the weekend at Carrizo Plain National Monument in Central California. I anticipated driving about 55 miles on dirt roads in my sedan over the weekend, and I brought along 2 cans of tire repair aerosol just in case. Carrizo Plain National Monument is the largest grassland in California, but also has a desert feel in parts and a dry alkaline lake. It's a great example of the variability of the California landscape.

I started out by visiting a section of the San Andreas fault line, which is responsible for earthquakes throughout California. It looked like a small ridge followed by a depression before the plains continued around it, however knowing this was more to this sight than meets the eye put me in awe. An interpretive sign said that the fault is moving 1.3 inches a year, about as fast as fingernails grow, and that if I were to stand in that spot for 10 million years, I would be next to San Francisco's Golden Gate.

My main reason for visiting the area was to get another chance at seeing pronghorn. These are the "antelope" mentioned as playing in the "Home on the Range" song. However, they're not antelope and don't have any close living relatives. They are fascinating creatures. Their "horns" aren't true horns and aren't true antlers. Horns are cartilage and don't fall off, whereas antlers are bone and fall off and regrow every year. Pronghorn have two bones protruding from their heads and males grow black pronged cartilage sheaths over these bones, which fall off and regrow every year.

Pronghorn are the second fastest animal in the world after modern-day cheetahs, and they're far faster than any predator around today. Why all this extra speed? Because pronghorn evolved at a time when they had to escape from the now-extinct American cheetah. The cheetah has disappeared from North America, but the pronghorn are still running. Despite their speed, they can't jump very well, so pronghorn-friendly fences with space for them to crawl under have been installed in the area. They're also flighty and will run away easily, making them quite elusive.

Young pronghorn take time to develop their speed, so they spend much of their time laying down to hide from predators in the grass until they're fast enough to evade them. These young pronghorn are very cute, but looks can be deceiving. They're actually fratricidal killers. During pregnancy, around seven embryos normally develop inside a female pronghorn. The embryos each develop a pointy tip, which they use to stab the other embryos in the womb until only two are left alive. Female pronghorn almost always then proceed to give birth to twins, the victors in a fight to the death, survival of the fittest.

Pronghorn populations are struggling throughout much of their prior territory due to habitat fragmentation, so they're often reintroduced into areas with varying success. Here's wishing for a bright future for this unique American animal.

As I was hiking throughout the weekend, I was constantly scanning the foreground and horizon for pronghorn. But, there was another unique animal in the area that deserves attention, the giant kangaroo rat. Giant kangaroo rats and kangaroo rats live in deserts and grasslands and were both endangered until recently, when kangaroo rats were delisted. Giant kangaroo rats are still endangered, but are slowly making a comeback. I caught a quick glimpse of several of them running and jumping along the trail, with their big, powerful hind legs and long tail with fluff on the end of it.

I've also been fortunate enough to see kangaroo rats in the desert. They're true desert specialists who can survive almost entirely without water, extracting it from their food and using their kidneys to reduce and concentrate their urine. But, that's not all. Kangaroo rats can chemically metabolize water from the hydrogen in their food and the oxygen in the air. Incredible!

I spent some time looking for pronghorn near water sources on the plains. It was a very hot day and I thought they'd have to drink eventually, but no luck. So, I started to hike to higher, cooler elevations, thinking they might be seeking shelter from the heat up there. I was hiking up a steep, overgrown slope and was using my trekking pulls to try to push vegetation out of my way. However, my legs got tangled up in the trekking poles and vegetation, and I fell forward. I caught myself and I thought I was fine until one of my insulated water bottles with cold water fell out of the pocket on the side of my pack and crashed directly on my finger. Blood started flowing immediately. I took care of myself and gathered myself and my belongings together. Fortunately, my water hadn't rolled down the slope.

I finished my search at higher elevations without luck and made my way down to the plains. I pulled out some binoculars and started scanning the horizon. I saw some elk, which was exciting, but I continued with my focus on finding pronghorn. I returned to my car, drove farther south, and got out to scan the horizon with binoculars once more.

I saw an animal far out on the horizon which I thought might have been a pronghorn. I could sort of see its horns, and thought it was a male. I could see a white tail or spot on the back of the animal, but I couldn't make out the typical pronghorn fur pattern. Maybe it was a deer or an elk. I kept watching it and saw a female stand up out of the grass with a fawn. I was happy to see a family and thought they might be pronghorn, but I couldn't really tell. I was frustrated and didn't know what to think. I decided to call it a day.

The next morning I started early and saw the elk again as the sun was coming up. Overnight, I had realized these weren't ordinary elk, these were tule elk. This species of elk lives only in California. They were killed off for protein, tallow, and hides during the Gold Rush and were reintroduced throughout the state after a single group of tule elk was found in a drained swamp near Bakersfield. All modern tule elk are descended from this group. Groups of females, called harems, gather together with a single male, who defends the harem from other bulls with his large antlers. During their seasonal rut in the fall, the females go into estrus and breeding commences.

Tule Elk (the male is toward the right)

Hunters of elk sometimes refer to them as "ghosts of the forest" because they are so elusive, so I felt particularly happy to see this unique elk, which is such an important part of California's history.

I returned to the area where I thought I might have seen pronghorn the day before and the same family was there again, this time with some additional females. They were closer to the road this time and I was able to clearly see them through binoculars and confirmed they were pronghorn. My search had paid off! I tried to get some photos of them, even attempting to take a photo through my binoculars, but they were still too far away to get clear pictures. So, I just enjoyed watching their interactions with each other and their behaviors through my binoculars for a long time. I felt happy to have these special animals in the USA. I later saw a group of female pronghorn while driving through a grassland near Flagstaff, Arizona. But, this first family group of pronghorn I saw will always be special.

I had obtained a permit to visit a gated-off archaeological site in the area, and I headed there as the final stop on my trip. The site consisted of a giant sandstone formation with colorful pictographs from about 3,500 years ago painted onto it. Pictographs are painted onto the rock, whereas petroglyphs are chipped or scraped into the rock. The macaw image from earlier in this book was a petroglyph. You may have seen petroglyphs where black desert varnish is chipped away to reveal red sandstone beneath, which makes a striking sight.

Unfortunately, the site had a lot of vandalism, some of which dated back many years. I saw someone had scratched their initials into one of the more beautiful panels of pictographs along with the date "7.5.25". It was unclear if this referred to 1925 or 1825. I remembered visiting a pictograph panel in Utah made by the "Archaic people" who lived in the area between 8,000 and 2,000 years ago and about whom we don't know much else. The original floating figures had feet added to them sometime in the thousands of years separating us from their original creation. I could tell a difference in the hue of the paint used, but the feet were not recent creations. That alteration felt different from the initials and date at this pictograph site and it wasn't just that the Utah graffiti was from further back in time. I don't know the motivation for making either alteration, but adding feet didn't obliterate the original art. Perhaps the feet were added for spiritual reasons to "ground' ghosts, or perhaps they were merely added to have fun. It's human nature to want to leave our mark, but putting your initials and date over the top of ancient petroglyphs seems to be a very egotistical move that harms the future enjoyment of the original art and the ability of others to connect with the past. Although art is always reimagined, reinterpreted, and remixed, I'd recommend leaving pictographs and petroglyphs alone and refraining from touching them so that they will be around for future generations to appreciate.

Carrizo Plain Pictographs

I was later able to find some black and white photographs of the pictographs at the site which seem to be from the early 1900s and were taken using photographic plates. The photographs appeared in the book "Petroglyphs of California and Adjoining States" by Julian H. Stewart (the book notes it uses the term "petroglyphs" to refer to both petroglyphs and pictographs). It's not clear the exact date that the photographs were taken, but the introduction to the book notes that the information and photographs within were pulled from various sources and donated by various individuals. The book was published in 1929, but the section on the Carrizo Plain site quotes a letter from Arthur F. L. Bell in 1916 describing how the pictographs had deteriorated since his visit 13 years earlier, so the photographs might have come from one of those visits. Even though the letter speaks of deterioration, the photographs show a much less damaged site than what I experienced on my visit, and it made me sad to see how much vandalism has occurred since that time. Some of the pictographs even have bullet holes now. The initials and date I mentioned earlier do not appear in the photographs, so I imagine the photographs were taken before 1925, and that the initials were carved in 1925. Photography was invented in France in 1822, but the earliest surviving photograph we have is from 1826, so since the initials were missing from the photographs I found, they couldn't have been carved in 1825. The book isn't error-free, describing the sandstone formation as granite, but the photographic record it contains is impressive. The book is in the public domain, so I'm pleased to be able to share an image from it with you.

Similar View of Carrizo Plain Pictographs (probably from before 1925)

Archaeologists think the Carrizo Plain archaeological site contains pictographs done by the Chumash people. The Chumash lived on the Channel Islands off the coast of California, but also inhabited portions of the mainland. I saw a pictograph of the Chumash Sky Coyote symbol when I was onsite, but it wasn't until I was later home and looking at my photographs that I recognized what must have been a boat! Perhaps this was a representation of how the people traveled between the mainland and the Channel Islands all those years ago!

Suspected Chumash Boat Pictograph

*

The plains of the American Southwest are home to a couple of creatures that can give you a surprising scare, although they are harmless. The first of which is the black-tailed jackrabbit or American desert hare, which lives in deserts, scrublands, and grasslands. This hare hides so well among the bushes and grass that you don't realize it is there until you're right next to it. Then, the hare jumps out of hiding with its large ears standing on end and runs far away toward the horizon without stopping. The suddenness of the hare's appearance and escape and the fact that it doesn't stop when it's a safe distance away makes you feel as if you've just been pickpocketed by the hare and that it's trying to make a break for it with your wallet. The hare's large ears dissipate heat and allow it to stay cooler in hot environments.

The second creature to give a surprising scare is the New World quail, which is found in a wide variety of habitats including scrublands, grasslands, deserts, forests, and mountains. However, they tend to hide in bushes and grass in small groups called convoys until you're right next to them, at which point they explode into flight (called flushing), only to settle a short distance away. The sound and motion of these birds taking off all together gives the impression of a much larger animal, and has made me yell aloud on several occasions. Despite these short flights, these birds typically move through bushes and undergrowth by walking. Quail calls vary by species and are very unique. The California quail has a call that sounds like a sort of laugh shifting to a higher pitch with each repetition. "Ooo-haha, Ooo-haha, Ooo-haha!" The mountain quail has a loud, quick call that is easily heard over long distances. "Woo-loo-hoo!" I've heard mountain quail calling back and forth to each other across a valley in the evening, and it's a magical sound. Quails tend to be monogamous, at least within a season, and produce large broods.

Another bird with an interesting call, which is found in scrublands, grasslands, and deserts of the West, is the common poorwill, which is a relative of the eastern whip-poor-will found in the East. I read about this bird's call before actually hearing it, and when I finally heard it in person without having listened to an audio recording beforehand, I still knew it was a poorwill without question. It sounds like "poor-will-uh". The common poorwill is the only bird that will go into a state of torpor for up to months at a time when food is scarce or the weather is cold.

<u>Epilogue</u>

I hope you've enjoyed this sampling of my adventures in pursuit of what I've found to be America's most elusive wildlife. I'm so grateful for the experiences I've shared with you here, but this is certainly not the end of my search for animals, artifacts, and adventures in the wild!

In my hiking, focusing on one geographic region of the US rather than routinely hiking more broadly across the country or throughout the world has allowed me to get to know it more deeply. I've seen how things change throughout the seasons and how different plants and animals relate to each other and are related to one another. The American Southwest as a whole has become a place where I feel at home, and because it's such a diverse region, it's been an area where I've been able to search for iconic American animals that live throughout the country.

So far, I've learned the following lessons through my adventures. I think these lessons relate to one another and point to a way of relating to the world that is helpful.

Identity can bring problems. If we tell ourselves that we're the type of person who does this or we're not the type of person who does that, then we're creating a fixed reality in our minds. These fixed realities are at best oversimplifications of a complicated world. We're much more capable, adaptable, and flexible than we think and practice and the pursuit of desired changes brings more results than any inherent talent or attributes. If we remember this, we can use our identity as a tool to guide us rather than being confined by it.

Trust yourself and your judgment while being open to learning and improving your skills. Your brain is a wonderful organ that is constantly making sense of the world around you. It's not perfect, but we can trust in our own experience and judgment. Then, if we don't hold our identity too tightly, when we make a mistake we'll be open to change and growth.

Remember that conventions are just tools and don't perfectly reflect reality. If we learn to relate to things on multiple levels, then we'll be able to escape the trap of taking things in only one way and believing only one description of an event will reliably match reality. We might read about how a plant flowers at a certain time of the year and produces fruit at another and that might be a helpful guide, except when the plant doesn't follow that mold. Perhaps changes in altitude or precipitation or other unknown factors come into play. The fact that some animals are specialists who only live in narrow, niche environments doesn't negate the fact that animals will often show up in areas outside their defined habitats.

It's helpful not to get caught up in words. The phrase "Great American Desert" was originally used in the 1800s to describe the high plains to the east of the Rocky Mountains. The word "desert" used to refer to uninhabited, treeless land that was thought to not be useful for agriculture. It's ironic that today this region supports plenty of agriculture through irrigation. In modern times, the word "desert" has changed to indicate land that receives little precipitation, and it has a connotation of being a hot place (although deserts can certainly be cold). The phrase "Great American Desert" is now more likely used to describe a combination of the Sonoran, Mojave, Great Basin, and Chihuahuan deserts within the continental United States. However, there is nothing inherent in the phrase "Great American Desert" or even in the word "desert".

It's important to be observant and look deeply at the world around us and our own reactions to it. Really pay attention. Remember that emotions such as fear can be helpful pointers for our logical minds, but we shouldn't give ourselves over to them entirely. Being observant helps us to see things more clearly, which improves our judgment. Paying attention provides a settling and satisfying sense of place, which is perhaps not as common today for humans as it was in the past.

In our internal world, relating to our experiences on different levels is helpful. When I talked about my fear of heights and looking into the night sky, I described my ultimate freedom on one level and my conflicting internal tendencies on another level. This might seem like a contradiction and we might be tempted to flag the discrepancy and try to clarify things in concrete terms, to define a convention. However, doing so would squeeze away an important, ineffable insight. Relating to things on different levels doesn't mean that things aren't inherently true. On the contrary, it means truth is more complex than we think.

Learn to be comfortable with yourself and with others, and to make time for both. Alone time and time with those close to us are both important aspects of life. If we neglect one of these aspects, the other aspect also tends to be negatively impacted.

Putting the lessons we learn into practice in our lives is a daily commitment, but one worth pursuing. Lessons are not awards to put on the shelf, but new ways of acting. By putting the lessons and insights that we gather from our own experiences or the experiences of others into practice, we can see if they hold up or not. It's through this daily commitment that we can improve our lives and the lives of those around us.

I hope you find what you are passionate about, and get out there and pursue it.

A roadrunner puffs up its feathers on a chilly day to stay warm.

<u>**Author Bio**</u>

Daniel Toujours hikes, scrambles, and camps throughout the American Southwest. He racks up around 1,000 miles a year in pursuit of animals, artifacts, geologic marvels, and unique adventures. He feels most at home in the silence of the desert.

*

*

If you enjoyed this book, please consider writing a review on the bookseller's website to help others find this work. Thank you!

*

*